20th Century
PERSPECTIVES

The United Nations

Stewart Ross

Heinemann
LIBRARY

www.heinemann.co.uk
Visit our website to find out more information about Heinemann Library books.

To order:
 Phone 44 (0) 1865 888066
 Send a fax to 44 (0) 1865 314091
▢ Visit the Heinemann Bookshop at www.heinemann.co.uk to browse our catalogue and order online.

First published in Great Britain by Heinemann Library,
Halley Court, Jordan Hill, Oxford OX2 8EJ,
a division of Reed Educational and Professional Publishing Ltd.
Heinemann is a registered trademark of Reed Educational and Professional Publishing Ltd.

OXFORD MELBOURNE AUCKLAND
JOHANNESBURG BLANTYRE GABORONE
IBADAN PORTSMOUTH (NH) USA CHICAGO

Produced for Heinemann Library by Discovery Books Limited
Designed by Ian Winton
Illustrated by Stefan Chabluk
Consultant: Robert Hudson
Picture research by Rachel Tisdale
Originated by Dot Gradations
Printed by Wing King Tong in Hong Kong

ISBN 0 431 12005 6
06 05 04 03 02
10 9 8 7 6 5 4 3 2 1

British Library Cataloguing in Publication Data
Ross, Stewart, 1947
  The United Nations. – (20th century perspectives)
  1.United Nations – History
  I.Title
  341.2'3'09

Acknowledgements
The publishers would like to thank the following for permission to reproduce photographs:
Bettmann/Corbis pp. 6, 14; Corbis/Angelo Hornak p. 4; Corbis/Leif Skoogfors p. 18; Corbis/David & Peter Turnley p. 25; Corbis/Howard Davies pp. 26, 32; Hulton Archive Photos pp. 8, 9, 16, 23, 28, 29, 34, 35; Hulton Deutsch pp. 10, 19; Hulton Getty pp. 7, 20; Popperfoto pp. 12, 13 (Olivier Matthys), 21, 22, 24 (Eric Feferberg), 27 (Kanni Sahib); Popperfoto/Reuters pp. 5, 15, 31, 33, 37, 40, 41, 42, 43; Still Pictures pp. 30 (Mark Edwards), 36 (Shehzad Noorani), 38 (Shehzad Noorani), 39 (Herbert Giradet).

Cover photograph showing UN British battalion escorting humanitarian aid in the Balkans reproduced with permission of Hulton Getty.

Every effort has been made to contact copyright holders of any material reproduced in this book. Any omissions will be rectified in subsequent printings if notice is given to the publishers.

Any words appearing in the text in bold, **like this**, are explained in the glossary.

Contents

What is the United Nations?

On the east side of Manhattan Island, New York City, stands a huge rectangular block of a building overlooking the East River. Outside, bearing the emblems of almost two hundred nations, stands a long array of flagpoles. This is not US territory. It is a 7-hectare (18-acre) international zone – the headquarters of the United Nations, the most daring experiment in global co-operation ever undertaken.

The international club

The United Nations (UN) was founded in 1945 to promote world peace, assist peoples to determine their own future, and help develop social and economic well-being around the globe. It is not in any sense a world government. Instead, it is a meeting point, an organization bringing together just about all the independent nations of the world to help settle their differences and work together more closely.

The United Nations headquarters, New York. The skyscraper houses the administration, while the General Assembly meets in the building on the right.

The UN is like a club. The nations of the world join, pay some money as a subscription and get what benefits they can out of it. It is run by a permanent staff who manage its numerous branches. These specialize in matters like international law, **humanitarian** aid and peacekeeping. In the General Assembly of the UN the voice of the smallest nation can be heard alongside the most powerful, each having an equal say.

A chequered history

As we consider the global horrors that have occurred since the UN's founding – wars, massacres, famines, fearful destruction of the natural environment – we may wonder whether it has achieved anything. Indeed, the UN has many critics who condemn it for discussing much but achieving little. On the other hand, as we will see, despite its many failures the UN has chalked up many small but notable successes.

The history of the UN, therefore, is a mixed one. Established to preserve peace, it has spent more time trying to restore peace after fighting had broken out. Striving to eliminate poverty, it has seen the gap between the rich and poor nations grow ever wider. But would the world have been safer and fairer if the UN had never been set up? The question cannot be answered for certain, but the pages that follow will help you reach your own conclusion.

Guns and water – a UN peacekeeping soldier from Zambia gives water to Rwanda's Hutu refugees, 1995.

Purposes of the United Nations

The UN explained its purposes, as set out in its Charter, as follows:

- *to maintain international peace and security*
- *to develop friendly relations among nations*
- *to cooperate internationally in solving international economic, social, cultural and humanitarian problems and in promoting respect for human rights and fundamental freedoms*
- *to be a centre for harmonizing the actions of nations in attaining these common ends.*

The League of Nations

Men and women have long dreamed of creating a world in which peace and co-operation replace war and conflict. In 1595 the French Duke of Sully suggested a world army to keep global peace. In the next century the Quaker leader William Penn put forward the idea that the same aim could be achieved if everyone spoke the same language.

It was not until 1918, as the horrifying slaughter of World War One was nearing its end, that a statesman put forward a concrete plan for an organization to maintain world peace. The man was US President Woodrow Wilson and the organization he proposed became known as the League of Nations.

Created by the Treaty of Versailles in 1919 and based in Geneva, Switzerland, the League of Nations was in some ways similar to the

modern United Nations. It had an Assembly, in which all member nations had a vote, and a Council to keep the peace. Its large Secretariat (administration) undertook many **humanitarian** tasks, such as helping settle the huge number of **refugees** created by World War One and its peace settlements. Forty-two nations joined the League at its foundation.

President Wilson's dream

In January 1918 US President Woodrow Wilson announced to Congress 'Fourteen Points' to guide the post-world-war peacemakers. The last point sowed the seeds of the League of Nations, which, sadly, the USA never joined because the US Senate would not agree to it:
'A general association of nations must be formed under specific covenants [contracts] for the purpose of affording mutual guarantees of political independence and territorial integrity to great and small states alike.'

Troubles for the League

The League of Nations was seriously flawed. First, key nations did not join. The US Senate voted to keep the USA out of the League. Germany did not join until 1926 and the **USSR** (Union of Soviet Socialist Republics or Soviet Union) only became a member in 1934. Second, the League lacked 'teeth' – only by a **unanimous** vote could it act against a nation that broke the peace.

Italy, led by the **dictator** Benito Mussolini, invaded the Greek island of Corfu in 1923. The League huffed and puffed but was unable to put enough pressure on Mussolini to make him withdraw. He did eventually, but only after Greece had paid him considerable compensation. Force had triumphed, the League had failed.

The Corfu incident highlighted the League's weakness. This was further displayed in 1931 when Japan occupied the Chinese province of Manchuria, in 1935–36 when Mussolini invaded Abyssinia (Ethiopia), and in 1939 when **Nazi** Germany took over most of Czechoslovakia. On each occasion the League was unable to protect these countries. By the outbreak of World War Two in Europe (September 1939), the League of Nations was a disgraced institution.

A new beginning

Western leaders did not despair at the failure of the League of Nations. In 1941, before the USA had joined World War Two, US President Franklin D. Roosevelt met with the British Prime Minister Winston Churchill on board the battleship *Prince of Wales*, moored off the coast of Newfoundland. Surrounded by the paraphernalia of war, the two statesmen planned for peace. They drew up a document known as the 'Atlantic Charter'. It was a declaration of the principles of international politics that would be put in place after the war.

Beyond the Atlantic Charter

The Charter offered such principles as **free trade**, freely chosen governments and **disarmament** of the states whose aggression had led to World War Two (principally Germany, Japan and Italy). It also suggested an international security system be set up. The Charter's principles were later adopted by the United Nations.

Sowing the seeds of the United Nations – US President Franklin D. Roosevelt (left front) and British Prime Minister Winston Churchill (right front) meet on board the battleship Prince of Wales *in the western Atlantic, 1941.*

On 1 January 1942, 26 countries, including the **USSR** and the USA (by then in the war), signed a Declaration of the United Nations. The name 'United Nations' came from President Roosevelt. All those who signed the Declaration accepted the principles of the Atlantic Charter. From this point planning for a United Nations Organization was taken forward by the three major **Allied powers**, the USA, the USSR and the United Kingdom. Meanwhile, separate discussions began about setting up an **International Monetary Fund** and **World Bank**.

Difficulties and discussions

Agreement over the UN was not easy to find. The USSR, for example, wanted all of its constituent **republics** to have separate membership. Britain was worried that the UN would take away its overseas **colonies**. Another major problem was how votes were to be taken in the Security Council, the organization that would be responsible for preserving peace.

Eventually, after discussions in the USA at Dumbarton Oaks, Washington DC, (where China was also represented, 1944) and in the USSR at Yalta (1945), on 25 April 1945, just as World War Two was coming to an end, a United Nations Conference on International Organization gathered in San Francisco, California. Fifty nations were represented: nine from Europe, five from the **British Commonwealth**, three from the **communist** USSR (Russia, Ukraine and Belarus), 21 from the Americas, seven from the Middle East, three from Africa and two from East Asia. Poland, not represented at San Francisco, was later admitted as one of the 51 founder nations.

The UN is born

The aim of the Conference was to produce a charter setting out the basic principles and organization of the new United Nations Organization. Discussions lasted for two months. Eventually, on 26 June 1945, the UN Charter was ready for signing. It came into effect four months later, on 24 October 1945.

Reaching agreement – delegates from the major world powers – USA, USSR, United Kingdom, France and China – meet to sign up to the Charter of the United Nations, San Francisco, 1945.

The UN Charter

Influenced by the words of the American Constitution, the UN Charter begins:

'We the people of the United Nations determined to save succeeding generations from the scourge of war ... and to reaffirm faith in fundamental **human rights**, in the dignity and worth of the human person, in the equal rights of men and women and of nations large and small, and ... to unite our strength to maintain peace and security, and ... to employ international machinery for the promotion of the economic and social advancement of all peoples, have resolved to combine our efforts to accomplish these aims. Accordingly, our representative Governments ... have agreed to the present Charter of the United Nations and do hereby establish an international organization to be known as the United Nations.'

A world parliament

The central body of the United Nations, and the only one to which all members belong, is the General Assembly. This is a sort of world parliament, discussing a wide variety of issues from terrorism to child labour. The General Assembly meets once a year, between September and December, but it can be summoned for extra sessions in times of crisis.

The General Assembly first gathered in London. However, following rich American businessman John D. Rockefeller's donation of US$8.5 million towards buying the New York site, it was decided to build the headquarters there. This was a controversial decision. Many felt that the UN should be based in a neutral country like Switzerland, where the League of Nations had its headquarters.

UN membership

Membership of the UN was also controversial. At first, with the USA and the **USSR** locked in a Cold War, neither **superpower** was prepared to allow its enemy's friends and allies into the UN. The logjam was ended with a compromise in 1955, when sixteen new states were admitted. For

The world's parliament – the opening session of the UN General Assembly in September 1979. The Assembly is the only place where all nations, rich and poor, large and small, sit together as equals.

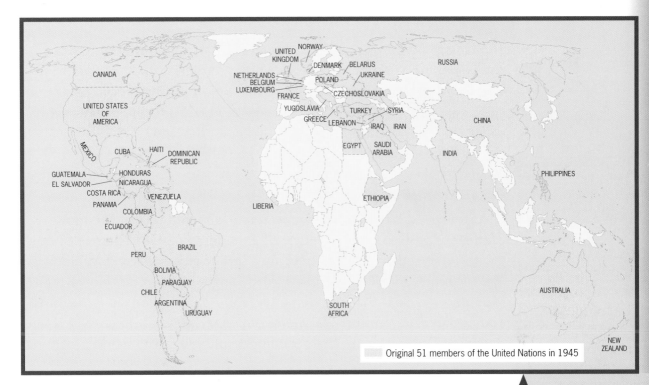

Original 51 members of the United Nations in 1945

example, the USA agreed to the membership of **communist** Hungary and Romania, while the USSR accepted the membership of US allies Spain and Ireland. Fifty new members were admitted between 1956 and 1968, many of them newly independent nations in Africa. A similar wave of new members came with the break up of the USSR in the early 1990s. Vietnam (1977) and Germany (1990) were reduced to single representation when North and South Vietnam and West and East Germany were reunited.

Language and meetings

Although there are six official UN languages – English, Chinese, French, Arabic, Russian and Spanish – all speeches are simultaneously translated into other languages.

The Trusteeship Council

The UN Charter set up the Trusteeship Council to look after eleven territories put under the protection of the UN in 1945. These territories, such as the Trust Territory of the Pacific Islands (formerly under the control of Japan), had belonged to powers defeated in World War Two. In 1994 the Trusteeship Council was suspended when the last Trust territory, Palau (in the Pacific Ocean) became independent.

The founding members of the United Nations. By 1957 most of the remaining countries of Europe and south-east Asia had also joined. As African states gained independence from 1955 to 1977 they too became members. In 1991–92 the UN expanded to include former Soviet republics in the Baltic and central Asia.

Struggling secretaries

The United Nations is run by its Secretariat, an administration that by the beginning of the 21st century employed almost 9000 people from 170 countries. They swear loyalty to the UN, rejecting special pleas from their own or any other country. As well as New York, the Secretariat has offices in Addis Ababa (Ethiopia), Bangkok (Thailand), Geneva (Switzerland), Nairobi (Kenya), Santiago (Chile) and Vienna (Austria).

An impossible job?

The Secretariat is headed by the secretary-general, one of the most prestigious posts in world politics. US President Franklin Roosevelt hoped the secretary-general would become a sort of global watchdog, alerting the Security Council to trouble and advising it what to do. However, it soon became clear that the best a secretary-general can do is **mediate** and advise. Austrian Kurt Waldheim (secretary-general, 1972–81) once described his position as 'the most impossible job in the world'.

The first secretary-general (1946–52), the Norwegian Trygve Lie, did his best to make his post one of real power and influence. In 1949, when Mao Zedong's **communists** took over the government of mainland China, the ousted pro-**Western** government of Jiang Jieshi fled to the island of Taiwan. With US backing, Jiang's government kept China's seat in the UN. Lie tried to get Chinese representation transferred to Mao's government but was prevented by the US which condemned him for 'taking sides'.

In 1950 Lie supported the Security Council's resolution for member states to help South Korea after it had been invaded by communist North Korea. It was now the turn of the **USSR**, North Korea's ally, to accuse Lie of 'taking sides'. In 1951 the Soviets **vetoed** Lie's reappointment. Facing fresh criticisms from the Americans, he resigned in 1952.

Swede Dag Hammarskjöld (1905–61), was the second secretary-general of the UN from 1953 to his death in 1961 in an air crash. Considered the 'founding father of UN peacekeeping' here he visits UN peacekeeping troops in Congo, July 1960.

Personal priorities

During the era of the Cold War similar difficulties were experienced by Lie's successors: Dag Hammarskjöld (Sweden, 1953–61), U Thant (Burma, 1961–71), Kurt Waldheim and Javier Pérez de Cuéllar (Peru, 1982–91). In 1967, for example, the USA accused U Thant of yielding to pressure from Egypt's President Nasser and removing the UN peacekeeping force from Sinai, the peninsula in north-eastern Egypt that borders Israel. In fact, he had no option: the force's presence required the agreement of the host country, Egypt.

The ending of the Cold War in 1990 freed the secretary-general from the need to balance the USA and the USSR. He gained little true freedom, however. When Boutros Boutros-Ghali (Egypt, 1992–96) tried to take a more active, independent line on international affairs, the US government objected. Understandably, in April 2001 the reforming secretary-general Kofi Annan (Ghana, 1997–2002; second term renewed to 2006) decided to avoid political involvement and made a campaign to tackle the HIV/AIDS epidemic his 'personal priority'.

The Ghanaian Secretary-General Kofi Annan (born 1938). Taking office in 1997, he worked hard to improve the way the UN was managed and run.

The secretary-general and the media

Secretary-General Boutros-Ghali struggled to prevent the US media from exerting too much control over the UN. Addressing the US press in 1995 he explained:

'We say we have sixteen members in the Security Council: the fifteen members plus **CNN**. Long-term work doesn't interest you [the media] because the span of attention of the public is limited. Out of twenty peacekeeping operations, you are interested in one or two ... And because of the limelight on one or two, I am not able to obtain the soldiers or the money or the attention for the seventeen other operations.'

International law and justice

*World justice?
The opening of
the Court of
International
Justice, took place
in The Hague,
Netherlands, in
1946.
International
justice is a fine
concept, but who
decides what
international law
is and who sees
that the court's
decisions are
carried out?*

The United Nations manages one permanent court, the International Court of Justice, or World Court. The International Court of Justice started as the Permanent Court of **Arbitration**, established in The Hague, Netherlands, in 1899 to hear international disputes. After working with the League of Nations, it came under the wing of the UN in 1946.

The World Court

The World Court hears disputes between member states, offering a judgement which all parties have agreed to accept (for example, on rights to drill for oil under the North Sea, 1969). It can also give an opinion at the request of individual states or an arm of the UN, such as the Security Council.

Unfortunately, less than half the UN members have been willing to accept the court's judgements. Moreover, most states are unwilling to bring political matters before the court. This is partly because the international law that the court interprets is uncertain and disputed. So, while the World Court performs worthwhile tasks, it has rarely caught the popular imagination.

Criminal courts

The same cannot be said of the UN's two criminal **tribunals** and its plans for a permanent international criminal court. In 1953, following the trials of **Nazi** and Japanese war criminals, the General Assembly called for the setting up of an international court to try people accused of **genocide**. The years passed, however, and nothing was done.

In the early 1990s plans for an international criminal court were revived. Two events led the UN into action: genocide in Bosnia and

Hercegovina (part of the former Yugoslavia) in the early 1990s and in Rwanda (central Africa), where hundreds of thousands of Tutsi people were massacred by the rival Hutus in a civil war in 1994. In 1993 the UN established the International Criminal Tribunal for Yugoslavia. The tribunal hit the world's headlines in 2001 when Yugoslavia's former president, Slobodan Milosevic, appeared before it. He was charged with **crimes against humanity**. Meanwhile, in 1994, an International Criminal Tribunal for Rwanda had been established to try Rwandan leaders accused of genocide.

Ex-president of Yugoslavia Slobodan Milosevic before the UN's War Crimes Tribunal in The Hague, Netherlands, 2001. In his defence he claimed that the court was illegal.

Following popular acceptance of these two tribunals, in 1998 the representatives of 160 UN nations agreed to create a permanent International Criminal Court at The Hague. The court would try crimes such as 'genocide, war crimes and crimes against humanity.' Secretary-General Kofi Annan hailed the move as 'a giant step forward in the march towards universal **human rights** and the rule of law'.

Against war criminals

The International Criminal Tribunal for Rwanda has the power to prosecute suspects accused of the following crimes against civilians:
a) murder
b) extermination
c) enslavement
d) deportation
e) imprisonment
f) torture
g) rape
h) persecutions on political, racial and religious grounds
i) other inhumane acts.

The Security Council

Many of the United Nation's more exciting moments take place in the Security Council, not the General Assembly. The latter tends to be a place of endless speeches aimed at people back home as much as those in the chamber. It is in the Security Council, the body that the UN Charter made responsible for international peace and security, that most important decisions are made.

The Security Council originally comprised eleven members – five permanent (USA, **USSR**, United Kingdom, France and China) and six temporary who served for two years. This arrangement was revised in 1965, when the number of temporary members rose to ten, selected to give balanced geographical representation. In the 1990s negotiations were started for Germany and Japan to become additional permanent members of the Security Council.

Where the mighty meet – the UN Security Council in session, January 1946. Because the permanent members of the Council could veto any decision, for years the Council rarely took a decisive action.

The use of force

A major weakness of the League of Nations had been its inability to back up its resolutions with armed force. So the UN would not suffer in the same way, it was hoped that the Security Council would be able to call upon a permanent force provided by member nations.

From the outset the USA and the USSR could not agree about this force. The Soviets wanted twelve **infantry divisions**, for example, while the USA wanted twenty. In the end there was no agreement. Consequently, whenever the UN needs armed forces they are provided for a specific mission only by willing member nations.

Two phases

The history of the Security Council (indeed, of the entire UN) since 1945 divides into two distinct parts. Until 1990 the Security Council was made powerless by a clause in the UN Charter that gave any one of the Council's five permanent members a **veto** over all major decisions. This was officially known as the 'Great Power Unanimity Rule'. UN plans to approve the use of force against an aggressor were vetoed by either the USSR (head of the **communist** world) or the USA (leader of the **democratic-capitalist** world).

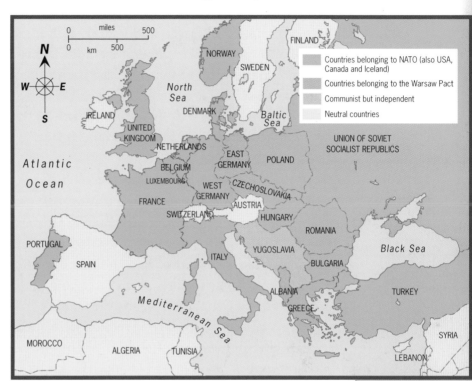

Europe at the time of the Cold War, 1947–90. The continent was divided between communism (mostly the Warsaw Pact countries) and capitalist-democracy (mostly the members of NATO).

After 1990, with the collapse of the USSR and the emergence of Russia as a democratic-capitalist state, it looked as if the Security Council might be able to work as intended in 1945. It flexed its new US-powered muscles almost immediately with the Gulf War of 1991.

The Cold War

America and the USSR fought as uneasy allies in World War Two. From 1946 onwards, fed by mutual misunderstanding and fear, relations between the two superpowers worsened. They never went to war but fuelled limited wars between other states. This period of frightening global tension, which lasted until 1990, is known as the 'Cold War'. America and its allies formed a military alliance, the North Atlantic Treaty Organization (NATO). The USSR and its communist supporters were members of an opposing military and economic alliance, the Warsaw Pact.

Working for peace

The first purpose of the United Nations, as set out in its Charter, is 'to maintain international peace and security'. This is a massive and, some say, impossible task. Nevertheless, it is vital and the UN is the only world body equipped to undertake it.

The maintenance of peace and security falls under two main headings, general and specific. The general includes the very existence of the UN – bringing people together to discuss their problems. It also involves **disarmament** and arms limitation, action to get rid of many of the causes of conflict, such as poverty and lack of education, and spreading a general acceptance of basic **human rights**.

Investigating conflicts, using force

Specific action to maintain peace was set out in Chapters Six and Seven of the UN Charter, giving powers mainly to the Security Council. The 1945 San Francisco conference imagined a scale of peace-keeping measures. These would rise from the **pacific**, such as investigating tense situations, to the **coercive**, such as sending UN troops into the field against a country that attacks another.

UN **arbitrators** were soon at work in the Middle East (after the establishment of Israel in 1947) and in Kashmir (after the independence of India and Pakistan, 1948). In the 1950s Secretary-General Dag Hammarskjöld introduced a peacekeeping role for the UN, one that was not in the Charter. It involved sending in neutral UN troops, with the agreement of both sides in a conflict (and the two **superpowers**, the USA and the **USSR**), to hold a line between the combatants. These forces were effective in a variety of war zones, from Congo to Cyprus.

UN soldiers of UNPROFOR (UN Protection Force for Former Yugoslavia), wearing their distinctive blue helmets, in Bosnia, 1995. The UN was criticized for not being prepared to use sufficient force to keep the peace.

Intervention?

An important provision in the Charter prevented the UN from intervening in the internal affairs of any state. This raised the difficult question of independence movements: peoples that claimed to be independent but were not recognized as such by a governing power.

True to its Charter, the Security Council refused to be drawn into conflicts in Northern Ireland (part of the United Kingdom, 1968 onwards) and Chechnya (part of the **Russian Federation**, 1994 onwards) but played an active role in Bosnia and the other newly independent states that emerged after Yugoslavia had broken up in 1991.

The best and the worst

Secretary-General Kofi Annan offered this eloquent defence of UN peacekeeping:

'The first United Nations peacekeeping operation [Congo, 1960] was an attempt to confront and defeat the worst in man with the best in man: to counter violence with tolerance, might with moderation, and war with peace. Since then, day after day, year after year, UN peacekeepers have been meeting the threat and reality of conflict, without losing faith, without giving in, without giving up.'

An Indian soldier of UNEF (United Nations Emergency Force) that entered Egypt in 1956. This was the UN's first true peacekeeping (as opposed to observation) force.

Uniting for peace

According to the UN Charter, the General Assembly may 'discuss any questions relating to the maintenance of international peace and security' and make recommendations to the Security Council or member states. In 1950 the Assembly went further than this with a 'Uniting for Peace' resolution. This allowed it to take over the Security Council's role (even calling for UN troops) if the **veto** prevented the Council from acting. The resolution was used several times during the 1950s, notably when the Assembly called for a UN Emergency Force for Suez (1956), where invading British and French troops, aided by Israel, opposed the Egyptian government's **nationalization** of the Suez Canal.

Enforcement

On a few occasions the United Nations approves the use of force to see its will obeyed. As the UN has no army or military commanders of its own, these enforcement actions are not under direct UN control. Instead they are undertaken by certain countries with UN approval. In 1999, for example, a force led by Australia and supported by troops from 21 other member states entered East Timor. Their task was to restore law and order after violence had flared between East Timorese seeking independence (with UN backing) and Indonesian forces unwilling to recognize East Timor's independence. Another example was the Gulf War against Iraq in 1991, which was led and largely conducted by the USA. After 1990 the UN also undertook smaller-scale enforcement actions (involving only a few hundred troops) in Somalia (1992–95), Rwanda (1993–96), Haiti (1993–94), and Bosnia and Hercegovina (1992–95).

Bypassing the veto

The outstanding example of an enforcement action undertaken in the name of the UN was the Korean War, 1950–53. At the end of World War Two, Korea was liberated from Japanese occupation by two armies, Soviet in the north and American in the south. Korea was consequently split between a Soviet-backed north and a US-backed south. **Superpower** forces withdrew in 1949. A year later **communist** North Korea, equipped with Soviet arms, launched a massive surprise attack on the South.

Evening assault – US forces, fighting in the name of the UN, attack the North Koreans at Inchon, September 1950.

The USA immediately sent troops to the South. At the same time it called on the Security Council to authorize UN action against the North Korean aggressors. Normally the **USSR** would have **vetoed** any Security Council decision to intervene. On this occasion, however, the Soviets were **boycotting** the UN.

They had withdrawn in protest at Taiwan, not the **People's Republic of China**, being the Chinese representative.

In the absence of the Soviet delegation, a resolution recommending member states to take action against North Korea was approved. This was the only time that the UN approved major enforcement action during the Cold War.

The Korean War

Although the US provided the bulk of foreign troops in South Korea, sixteen other nations, including the United Kingdom, Australia, New Zealand and Turkey, also sent contingents. At first the South Koreans and their allies were driven back to the south-east of the Korean peninsula.

They then counter-attacked and advanced all the way to the border with communist China in the north. At this point the Chinese intervened and pushed the South Koreans back to the border between North and South Korea. Here the fighting became bogged down, until eventually it ended in July 1953.

Korea remained divided. The North had lost perhaps a million men, China some 500,000, South Korea 600,000 and the UN 57,000 (of whom 54,000 were Americans). In contrast to the League of Nations, which was never able to organize powerful countries to take action against aggression, the UN had shown that it could defy aggression by approving superpower action. On the other hand, the Soviet Union learned from its mistake and made sure that in future it was represented at Security Council meetings.

The Korean War (1950–53): American troops, fighting for the UN, resist an assault of Chinese troops. The war was the only time during the Cold War when forces went into battle in the name of the UN.

The blue helmets

Between 1948 and 2002 the United Nations launched 54 peacekeeping operations, 41 of them after 1990. Although the Security Council sets up and plans peacekeeping missions, the secretary-general is responsible for their management and for directing operations. More than 120 states make military and civilian personnel available, and even Switzerland, one of the few countries that isn't a member of the UN, provides money and equipment.

These statistics are impressive. Nevertheless, particularly before 1990, the presence of UN peacekeepers (who wear blue helmets) was rarely more than a token. Where they became involved in fighting, as in Congo, the result was disastrous. Learning from that experience, later peacekeeping operations generally avoided involvement in conflicts and consequently were more successful.

Congo

One of the first UN peacekeeping forces (called ONUC) entered the newly independent **Republic** of Congo (later Zaire, now Democratic Republic of Congo) in 1960. It came at the request of the Congolese prime minister, with the backing of the Security Council, to try to restore peace after civil war followed independence from Belgium.

UN troops wait patiently to board a plane going to Congo in about 1961. Their prescence created mixed feelings.

Hardly had ONUC become active than it found itself at the centre of a political storm. It was resented by many Congolese and even UN Secretary-General Hammarskjöld said **Western** nations were using it to do 'their dirty work in Congo'. By this he meant that he believed UN forces were supporting Western (especially Belgian) businesses, such as mining, in Congo. The **USSR** also believed that the UN was protecting Western interests and it refused to pay for the mission. ONUC withdrew in 1964 and the fighting continued until the victory of the rebel leader Joseph Désiré Mobutu in 1965.

Cyprus

In 1964 the Security Council sent in a UN force, UNFICYP, to the Mediterranean island of Cyprus. Its brief was to keep the peace between the minority Muslim Turks and the majority Christian Greeks (80 per cent of the population). However, when Turkish forces invaded in 1974 (to protect the Turkish minority) and seized the northern part of the island, UNFICYP was powerless to resist them. The island remains divided to this day, with UNFICYP troops still patrolling its frontier.

El Salvador

With the end of an eleven-year civil war in El Salvador (Central America) in 1992, a UN force, ONUSAL, entered the country. Comprising both military and civilian personnel, its task was to see that the cease-fire agreed between the two sides (the **right-wing** government and its **left-wing** opponents) stuck; that various reforms – including fair trials, greater rights for women and minority racial groups, land distribution and help for the poor – were carried out; and that free and fair elections were held. Three years later ONUSAL had successfully fulfilled its tasks and was disbanded.

Just watching – a Canadian UN observer in Cyprus, 1964. When the Turks invaded the island ten years later the UN troops could offer no resistance.

Modern failure

The ending of the Cold War and the new spirit of cooperation that this brought to the Security Council did not mean all UN peacekeeping missions were successful. In 1993, for instance, a UN force, UNOSOM II, was sent to Somalia, an east African country torn by civil war and famine. The UN force was instructed 'to take appropriate action, including enforcement measures, to establish throughout Somalia a secure environment for **humanitarian** assistance'. On meeting with fierce armed resistance, in 1994 UNOSOM II was told to cease military action. It was withdrawn a year later.

The Gulf War

Many hoped the ending of the Cold War would usher in a period of peace and justice. Without two **superpowers** to support opposing sides, it was hoped that international conflicts would be more easily resolved. Moreover, freed from the Security Council **veto**, the United Nations would be able to make the world a safer place. The Gulf War seemed to support such optimistic judgements.

Invasion of Kuwait

In 1990 Iraq's President Saddam Hussein accused his small but oil-rich neighbour Kuwait of producing too much oil. Over-production, he claimed, was forcing down the price of oil. He also said that some of Kuwait's oil came from wells inside Iraqi territory.

Iraq invaded Kuwait on 2 August and formally **annexed** it a few days later. The **West**, which had previously supported Saddam Hussein, was worried lest he move from Kuwait to neighbouring Saudi Arabia, the world's leading oil producer.

Trying to find a peaceful solution – following Iraq's invasion of Kuwait in August 1990, UN Secretary-General (1982-92) Pérez de Cuéllar (left) talks with Iraqi minister Tarek Aziz.

UN action

The government of the **USSR** was breaking up at this time and its diplomats did not oppose the West's views. In these circumstances, the USA and its allies had little trouble persuading the Security Council to back action against Iraq. **Economic sanctions** were applied. When these produced no response, a resolution approving the use of 'all necessary means' was agreed. It was not a formal call for force. Nevertheless, the USA and her allies interpreted it as supporting military action.

A multinational force, largely US (500,000 military personnel), was assembled in Saudi Arabia. Military operations – codenamed 'Desert Storm' – began in January 1991 with a devastating six-week bombing campaign. Troops operating in the name of the UN crossed into Kuwait on 24 February. Four days later, when a cease-fire was called, they had liberated Kuwait and were advancing deep into Iraq.

A new era?

From the UN point of view the Gulf War appeared a great success. Against Iraq's losses of some 110,000 soldiers and 10,000 civilians, the Allies had lost only 343 military personnel. Kuwait had been freed, aggression thwarted and collective security (nations pooling resources to combat aggression) shown to work – a bright new era in UN history seemed to be dawning.

Gulf War, 1991 – troops take aggressive action in the name of the UN for the first time since Korea, 40 years earlier.

Others were less optimistic. They pointed out that Desert Storm's success had depended not on collective security but on the West's determination to protect its supply of cheap oil. They argued that had Saddam moved against another neighbour – Iran, Syria or Jordan, for example – the allies would almost certainly not have reacted so strongly. Furthermore, the Security Council's backing had depended more on the USSR's weakness than support. In other words, the circumstances of the Gulf War were quite similar to those of the Korean War.

Disarmament and arms limitation

The application of modern technology to armaments in the 19th century produced a double problem: the new weapons were terrifyingly destructive and used up a huge amount of a country's wealth in their production. Out of this situation the modern **disarmament** movement was born.

Individual states agreed arms limitation treaties but more widespread disarmament was more difficult to achieve. International disarmament conferences were held in 1899, 1907 and, under the League of Nations, 1932–34. All failed to reach agreement.

Old cause, old difficulties

After the first use of **nuclear weapons** at the end of World War Two, the United Nations took up the arms control cause. Article Eleven of the Charter empowered the General Assembly to investigate the matter, and Article Twenty-six asked the Security Council to draw up 'a system for the regulation of armaments'.

A Disarmament Commission was founded in 1952. Geneva hosted UN disarmament negotiations from 1962 to 1978. Meanwhile, various UN armament agreements were drawn up. These banned, for example, the testing of nuclear weapons (1963), **weapons of mass destruction** on the sea bed (1970) and the manufacture and use of chemical weapons (1993).

Not surprisingly, the UN-sponsored efforts had little real effect. The problems were much as before. Governments feared that large-scale disarmament would destroy their important armament industries, bankrupting many and making millions unemployed. Arms reduction would have similar but less catastrophic consequences.

Governments that dreamed of conquest or feared attack were also unwilling to disarm. Even if they agreed, they argued, who would make the first move and who would monitor the process? The same arguments applied to arms reduction. A good example of the sort of problems the UN encountered came early on, in 1946. The UN wanted nuclear weapons reduced in number or even eliminated entirely. The USA agreed, but said it would destroy its weapons only after an international system of weapons control was agreed. The **USSR** (which at that time did not possess nuclear weapons but was working hard to develop them) said the destruction of nuclear warheads should come before agreement on a system of control. The result: deadlock and the continuing nuclear threat.

Over disarmament and arms reduction, therefore, the UN found itself in the same position as on other issues: it had no independent power. Ultimately, it could do only what its members agreed to do. Its chief role was to **mediate** and encourage. Even when it oversaw the production of a **convention** or **treaty** (such as the 1968 Treaty on the Non-**Proliferation** of Nuclear Weapons in which the USA, the Soviet Union and the United Kingdom agreed not to help other countries develop nuclear weapons), it could not guarantee that states would endorse it. France and China, both major nuclear powers, did not sign up to the Non-Proliferation of Nuclear Weapons Treaty until 1992.

UN weapons inspectors leave their headquarters in Baghdad. Charged with finding and destroying Iraq's weapons of mass destruction, the UN team was eventually harassed into withdrawing.

The UN and Iraq

After the Gulf War the Security Council banned Iraq from making or holding weapons of mass destruction and set up a Special Commission, UNSCOM, to oversee the destruction of such weapons in Iraq. Meanwhile, the UN imposed sanctions that allowed Iraq to sell only such oil as was needed to support its people. Saddam Hussein claimed the sanctions caused unnecessary suffering. He continually hampered UNSCOM's work. It withdrew in 1998 and was replaced by another commission, UNMOVIC, in 1999. Ten years after the Gulf War the UN and Iraq were no nearer resolving their differences.

Closing the gap

The United Nations was never intended to be simply a peace-preserving body. Its 1945 Charter provided it with an Economic and Social Council (ECOSOC), whose function was to co-ordinate and supervise the UN's economic and social work. Interestingly, as the UN's peacekeeping and disarmament role ran into difficulties, its economic and social role expanded. As a result, by the end of the 20th century, ECOSOC was taking 85 per-cent of the UN budget and its work was touching many times more lives than that of the Security Council.

Expanding role

When ECOSOC was founded in 1945 it had just eighteen members, elected by the General Assembly for three years. Fifty years later the membership had risen to 54, representing more than a quarter of all UN member countries. The reason for this increase is the huge variety of work undertaken by ECOSOC, ranging from tackling the problem of illegal drugs to monitoring the status of women world-wide.

Helping the children – UNICEF (United Nations International Children's Emergency Fund) provides free food and drink for the people of Vienna, Austria, April 1948.

The Council, which divides its time between New York and Geneva, supervises nine commissions (for example the Commission on Crime Prevention and Criminal Justice and the Commission on Human Rights) and five Regional Commissions (for example the Economic and Social Commission for West Asia). It also works with a vast number of other UN committees, organizations, programmes and agencies. These include the United Nations International Children's Emergency Fund (UNICEF), the World Health Organization (WHO) and, most controversial of all, the United Nations Educational, Scientific and Cultural Organization (UNESCO).

UNICEF

The United Nations International Children's Emergency Fund (UNICEF) was created in 1946 to help European children after World War Two. It became permanent in 1953. UNICEF works with governments, charities and other organizations to help children the world over. Its particular concerns are promoting education, health and well-being for all children, regardless of gender, religion or race. It wants all children to live in dignity and security. UNICEF is particularly famous for its greetings cards which it sells to raise funds for its many projects.

The Commission on Sustainable Development

The Commission on Sustainable Development (CSD) was founded in 1992 and has been one of ECOSOC's successes. After the 1992 Earth Summit in Rio de Janeiro, Brazil, the CSD was charged with monitoring the progress of agreements made at the summit and advising on a wide range of environmental issues. Its overall aim was to produce during the 21st century a plan for world economic development that did not harm the environment. As concern for the environment grew, so did interest in the CSD's work. Its meetings attracted over 50 government ministers and delegations from hundreds of other organizations around the world.

UNESCO

Secretary-General U Thant, speaking in 1968, said of the ECOSOC network that 'for the first time in history, [it] provided mankind with mechanisms that would seek to improve the life of every man, woman and child on earth.' Sadly, such work is inevitably wrapped up with politics and therefore highly controversial. No organization reflects this more than UNESCO.

In 1945 the USA had perhaps been UNESCO's most eager supporter. It believed the organization would promote peace through education and understanding. However, by the 1970s UNESCO had come under the control of **Third World radicals** who claimed that all news and information was distorted because it came through **Western**-owned media organizations. UNESCO's director-general, Amadou-Mahtar M'Bow of Senegal, seemed more concerned with who owned the press than with its freedom.

Basic needs – children in Haiti write on a blackboard provided by UNESCO, 1949.

UNESCO's anti-Western political statements, inefficiency and **corruption** infuriated the USA, which met a quarter of the organization's budget. When M'Bow refused to reform, the USA walked out of UNESCO in 1984, followed by the United Kingdom a year later. Some of the advisors to Ronald Reagan (the US president at the time) even advised that the USA leave the UN altogether.

World health

With the birth of modern medicine by the early 20th century, charitable attempts were made to make its benefits available to everyone. Wealthier nations realized, too, that it was in their self-interest to stamp out disease in less developed parts of the world to prevent it spreading. To this end the International Office of Public Health was set up in Paris in 1907 and the League of Nations Health Organization in 1923. In 1948 the work of these two organizations was absorbed into a new agency of the United Nations, the World Health Organization (WHO).

WHO at work

The brief of the WHO was much broader than those of its two predecessors. Where they were primarily concerned with disease control, the WHO aimed at 'the highest possible level of health' for everyone. In other words, its programme sought positive mental, physical and social health and well-being, not just the absence of sickness. Behind this thinking lay the belief that ill-health, like poverty, lay behind much of the world's discontent and conflict.

The WHO launched its most ambitious campaign – 'Health for all by 2000' – at the end of the 1970s. It was, perhaps, an impossible dream. Certainly the health of the human race was better at the end of the 20th century than it had been 30 years before, but some 25 per cent of people still suffered from treatable illness. Moreover, no sooner had one illness been brought under control than another appeared. The most obvious example of a new and deadly sickness was AIDS, although in the wealthiest nations obesity (the state of being very overweight) was causing alarm. The WHO drew attention to obesity by collecting and publishing information on the problem.

Information, epidemics and advice

Much of the work of the WHO involves collecting and passing on information on health related matters. This means collecting statistics about the number of people suffering from malaria, for example, and keeping nations informed of the latest advances in cancer research.

World Health Organization workers measure children in Ivory Coast to discover the correct drug dosage needed to protect them from the disease onchoceriasis (river blindness).

SPREAD LOVE NOT AIDS

A second area of WHO work involves fighting **epidemic** diseases. This is done by funding and organizing vaccination programmes, educating national public health authorities and making improvements to the environment, such as providing pure water supplies.

The UN and AIDS

In many of its programmes the WHO works alongside other agencies. AIDS, for example, is too large a problem to be tackled by a single arm of the UN. The Joint United Nations Programme on HIV/AIDS (UNAIDS) linked the WHO with UNICEF, UNDP (the United Nations Development Programme), UNESCO, the World Bank and other agencies. Together they conduct research, collect information and advise how the epidemic may be controlled. Equally important, they also raise awareness about AIDS with information campaigns and by running an annual World AIDS Day.

Finally, the WHO spends much time and money helping construct effective health services in UN member states. The work involves training, advising, funding and assisting in every way possible so that, one day, each nation will be able adequately to care for the health of all its people.

Emergency!

Long before World War Two ended, the **Allied powers** realized that when the guns finally fell silent homes had to be found for the millions of **refugees** and reconstruction had to be started in countries devastated by war. Therefore, two years before the United Nations itself was founded, a United Nations Relief and Rehabilitation Administration (UNRRA) was formed. Its main aim was to help the millions of refugees in Europe and Asia.

Refugees

In 1947 the UN replaced UNRRA with the International Refugee Organization (IRO). This lasted only four years before it became the United Nations High Commission for Refugees (UNHCR), which began operating on 1 January 1951. Over the second half of the 20th century UNHCR helped an estimated 50 million people. Many, such as the Palestinians, Rwandans and Afghans, were made refugees by war. Others, such as the Ethiopians and African peoples living on the fringes of the Sahara Desert, were driven from their homes by famine and drought. Whatever the cause, UNHCR provided refugees with basic necessities – food and shelter – then did what it could to enable them to return home.

Helping the refugees – UN soldiers help Cambodians to return home, 1992. Many thousands had fled abroad to escape the bloodshed and tyranny of the 1970s and 1980s.

Getting it together

When disaster strikes, whether earthquake, flooding or war, there is usually an adequate supply of relief labour, goods and money. The governments of developed countries have all built up emergency relief programmes. These supplement the world-wide charities like Oxfam, the Red Cross and the Red Crescent. There are also the UN's own agencies – UNHCR, for example, the World Food Programme, UNICEF, WHO and others. The trouble is, getting all these groups to work together is almost impossible. During the famine in Ethiopia in the mid-1980s, for example, there were widespread reports of wastage, inefficiency and **corruption**.

The UN is the obvious body to co-ordinate major relief operations because it is the only international organization that has universal approval. However, not until 1997, when it established its Office for the Coordination of Humanitarian Affairs (OCHR), did

World Food Programme

Plans for a World Food Programme (WFP), sending emergency food supplies to where they were most needed, were drawn up in 1962. It was to operate on a three-year trial basis, starting in January 1963. Before the end of 1962, however, there was an earthquake in Iran, a hurricane in Thailand and Algeria was struggling to resettle 5 million refugees. In all three locations people were starving. The WFP started work before its official launch date and never stopped.

a reasonably efficient machinery come into being. By 2000 OCHR was raising US$1.4 billion to help 35 million distressed people in sixteen separate countries and regions.

Longer term

Natural disasters cannot be prevented. Nevertheless, steps can be taken to lessen their effect. So, as well as supplying immediate aid to those affected, the UN concentrates huge resources on helping societies recover and become less vulnerable to future disasters. This is the prime function of the United Nations Development Programme (UNDP). A huge undertaking, the UNDP is concerned with issues like promoting **democratic** government as well as crisis prevention and recovery.

Transport for the homeless – UN lorries arrive at the Mukaruka camp, Zaire, (now the Democratic Republic of Congo) to take back home Rwandan refugees who had fled the bloodshed in their own country, 1994.

33

Human rights

There had been talk of all human beings having basic rights since at least the 17th century. It was difficult to find agreement on what those rights were, however, and even more difficult to get governments and other authorities to respect them. The total lack of respect for **human rights** shown by several regimes of the mid-20th century (such as the persecution of Jews in **Nazi** Germany and of religious believers in the **USSR**) prompted United Nations pioneers to tackle the problem afresh.

The Universal Declaration

The UN Charter of 1945 spoke of human rights and three years later these were defined in a Universal Declaration of Human Rights (1948) adopted by the General Assembly on 10 December 1948. All member countries were urged to allow the text to be displayed and read in schools and other educational institutions.

The Declaration demands 'universal respect for and observance of a common standard of achievement for all peoples'. This is easier said than done. For example, Article Two of the Declaration says the rights applied equally to everyone, no matter what their 'race, colour, sex, language, religion, political or other opinion, national or social origin, property, birth or other status'. Yet some religious groups believe women inferior to men; others believe certain social groups (castes) are lower in status than others. Over such issues gender and social rights clearly conflict with religious rights.

Rights and reality

A UN Commission on Human Rights (UNCHR, established 1946) produced a stream of committees and declarations on rights-related subjects such as racism, women's rights, apartheid, the treatment of prisoners and slavery. In 1993 the post of UN High Commissioner for

Human Rights was created to give the rights movement sharper focus. Four years later the post was strengthened and given to the outstanding lawyer and retiring president of Ireland, Mary Robinson.

Even when headed by someone as high profile as Mary Robinson, UNCHR's effectiveness was limited. The Commission could put pressure on the government of Sudan (in north-east Africa) to end the custom of female circumcision because Sudan was a poor country needing all the UN help it could get. On the other hand, there was much less UNCHR could do to persuade the government of the oil-rich Saudi Arabia to extend human rights to its citizens.

Apartheid and South Africa

Apartheid means 'separate development'. It applied to the system established in South Africa after World War Two that treated its white, coloured and black races differently. Specifically, the whites were a privileged minority and other races deprived of basic human rights. UNCHR campaigned vigorously against apartheid. It did not get the support it might have hoped for from the West because South Africa was a powerful anti-**communist** force in southern Africa. This changed with the collapse of communism. By 1990 the West no longer needed the support of South Africa's all-white government, and apartheid was swiftly overturned.

The rights of women

When the United Nations was founded, talk of **human rights** centred around issues like fair trials, the right to vote and freedom of speech. By the 1960s the central rights issue had become race – specifically, outlawing racial prejudice. During the 1980s the focus changed again. The new rights issue was gender: the right of women to be treated equally with men.

New cause, new organizations

In the 1980s and 1990s the UN set up a vast range of women's groups. At the centre were the UN Division for the Advancement of Women (UNDAW), the UN Development Fund for Women (UNIFEM), and the International Research and the Training Institute for the Advancement of Women (INSTRAW). The call was taken up by existing UN organizations, such as UNICEF, UNESCO and WHO, all of whom started giving priority to women's issues.

In Bangladesh a group of women protest for women's rights on International Women's Day – a day organised by the UN.

The theme was also taken up by the Human Rights Commissioner, Mary Robinson, who declared in 1998, 'There can be no human rights without women's rights.' The UN organized world conferences on women. Special funds were set aside in developing countries specifically for women to start their own enterprises. At the same time, a huge amount of information on gender discrimination was made available in an attempt to shame people and governments into action. It showed, for example, that of the 400 cases of domestic violence reported in the Punjab, Pakistan, in 1993 almost half resulted in the death of the wife.

Successes and failures

As with so many causes taken up by the UN, there was much discussion but less specific action. All of the first signatories of the UN Charter were men. Over 50 years later, in 2001, it still bore the signatures of only

A huge dove of peace floats above the delegates to the UN's 4th World Conference on Women, held in Beijing, China, in 1995.

four women (from the Dominican Republic, USA, Brazil and China). Women were still second-class citizens in many countries, few were in high positions in government or commerce, and forced marriage and brutality were widespread. Statistics showed domestic violence to be increasing, although this may have been because it was being reported more often.

Despite this gloomy outlook, progress was made, thanks in large part to UN pressure. In 1991 Mexico changed its rape law to help women victims. Turkey, traditionally a male-dominated society, established a Ministry of State for Women. Brazil set up special police units to deal with women's issues. Of course, changing customs thousands of years old takes more than a decade. Nevertheless, by the 21st century the outlook for millions of women was certainly brighter than it had been twenty years earlier.

Advancing Women's Rights

From the Declaration of the UN Conference on Women, Beijing, 15 September 1995:

'We, the Governments participating in the Fourth World Conference on Women ... Recognize that the status of women has advanced in some important respects in the past decade but that ... major obstacles remain ... [and] Dedicate ourselves unreservedly to addressing these constraints and obstacles and thus enhancing further the advancement and empowerment of women all over the world.'

The environment

The United Nations has faced two forces that threaten global destruction. The first, which dominated for the first 25 years of the UN's existence, was nuclear war. By the later 20th century this threat had receded markedly. By then, however, it had been replaced by something more complex but equally worrying – environmental catastrophe.

The gathering disaster

By the mid–1980s reports were warning that human activity was seriously damaging the Earth's environment. Gases from refrigerators and aerosols were destroying the **ozone** layer in the upper atmosphere that protected the Earth from the sun's harmful rays. Industrial and domestic discharge was polluting rivers, seas and oceans. Millions of square miles of irreplaceable rainforest had disappeared.

Most alarming of all, the burning of fossil fuels (oil, coal, gas) was surrounding the Earth with a layer of heavy gases. These acted like the glass of a greenhouse, trapping the heat from the sun. This 'greenhouse effect' was causing global warming. The measurable rise in temperatures led to marked climate changes, expanding desert regions and melting polar icecaps, causing sea levels to rise. Widespread flooding was predicted.

The ozone layer – a UN success story

By the mid-1980s it was clear that the Earth's protective ozone layer was being depleted. In response the UN Environmental Programme brought together all industrialized nations to agree the Montreal Protocol (1987). This phased out the production and use of gases that harmed the ozone layer by 1996, saving millions from contracting potentially lethal skin cancer.

Enter the UN

Because environmental change is a truly global problem, the UN is the only organization equipped to deal with it. As with its other work, it can act only with the permission and support of

The horrors of climate change – global warming caused by pollution of the atmosphere is said to have been partly responsible for an increase in natural disasters. This severe flooding took place in Bangladesh in 1998.

its members. Here it runs into a major difficulty. The USA is both the largest contributor to UN funds and the major source of 'greenhouse' pollution. Its motor industry, a large-scale polluter, is a huge employer. Consequently, the UN faces perhaps the most serious danger in its history without the support of its richest and most powerful member.

The Earth Summit

Although it established an Environment Programme in 1972 (UNEP), the UN did not recognize the seriousness of the environmental situation until 1983, when it launched a World Commission on Environment and Development. This reported back to the General Assembly in 1987. What was needed, it said, was a major world-wide conference on the environment.

The UN Conference on Environment and Development (UNCED) – the 'Earth Summit' – finally met in Rio de Janeiro, Brazil, in 1992. Altogether, 178 governments were represented. After much talk, the Earth Summit produced a series of splendid sounding declarations. However, since it agreed no way of enforcing them, they were destined to remain largely expressions of goodwill.

US Vice-President Al Gore at the Rio de Janeiro Earth Summit, 1992. The summit was criticized for talking too much and doing too little.

Sustainable development

From the Rio Declaration on Environment and Development, 1992:
'... human beings are at the centre of concerns for **sustainable development**. They are entitled to, a healthy and productive life in harmony with nature ... States have a sovereign right to exploit their own resources but not to cause damage to the environment of other States.'

Kyoto

Poisoning our world – a dense layer of polluting smog hangs over the city of Santiago, Chile, in 1999. Protecting the environment is arguably the UN's greatest challenge of the 21st century.

By the time the nations of the world gathered again to discuss the environment, it was clear that the Rio Earth Summit had resulted in few concrete improvements. The most pressing need at the 1997 Earth Summit in Kyoto, Japan, was to find a way of making the 1992 United Nations Framework Convention on Climate Change (UNFCCC) work.

Three sides

The negotiating nations at Kyoto fell broadly into three groups. The majority belonged to developing states that caused relatively little pollution and did not want strict controls over their future industrial expansion. A second group, largely European, comprised the industrialized nations that were prepared to make the changes necessary to reduce the production of 'greenhouse gases'.

Finally, there were the USA, Australia and, to a lesser extent, the **Russian Federation** and Ukraine. They were suspicious about the suggested levels of greenhouse gas reduction. Instead, they questioned the reality of global warming and suggested using large areas of forest to absorb extra carbon dioxide (a greenhouse gas).

The Kyoto Protocol

The Kyoto negotiations were long and difficult. Eventually a **protocol** was drawn up – the world's developed countries pledged to reduce their overall average greenhouse gas output to 5 per cent below the 1990 level in 2008–12. Politicians hailed the agreement as a victory for common sense.

Environmentalists, however, saw it as no victory at all. Scientists had suggested a cut of over 50 per cent was needed. Although the Kyoto Protocol was legally binding, there was no mechanism to bring defaulters to court. Besides, how could one bring a country to court if it refused to sign the Protocol? The US, for example, pulled out of the agreement in 2001.

40

Trade in emission quotas

The Kyoto Protocol accepted the US government's idea of nations 'trading' emissions. This allowed countries or companies to buy permission to emit pollutants. The seller was a country that had cut pollution more than it was required to do. The trading meant that a wealthy state or business could buy its way out of meeting its Kyoto undertaking.

Different situation, same problem

The Kyoto Protocol highlighted the strengths and weaknesses of the UN. It had identified a serious global problem, assembled the nations of the world to discuss it and presented them with a viable plan. In the end, though, it could make nothing happen on its own. It could do only what its members, particularly its more powerful members, would agree to.

The threat of **nuclear weapons** could be ended by destroying them. Destruction of the environment could not be dealt with so simply. By the 21st century it had become the UN's sternest test. If it succeeded, future generations would owe it an everlasting debt. If it failed, the prospect was not worth contemplating.

Kyoto, Japan, December 1997. After much discussion, delegates attending this UN-organized conference on climate change agreed a treaty to halt climate change. Five years later, many countries had still not put the treaty into effect.

Protest!

Many Americans did not agree with their government's attitude towards the Kyoto Protocol. In 2001 the environmental group Save Our Environment asked its followers to send this letter to President George W. Bush:
'I strongly oppose your decision not to regulate carbon dioxide emissions from the nation's power plants, and to pull the US out of the Kyoto Protocol ... Rather than rely on sound science and cost-effective solutions to the nation's environmental and energy needs, you have chosen to bolster fossil fuel interests that pollute our air and water and contribute further to global warming.'

Past and future

The United Nations has reflected the world, not moulded it. Any hopes that it would do otherwise were soon dashed in the tensions that led to the Cold War. Therefore, any criticism of the UN and its shortcomings is in part a criticism of ourselves, the nations of the world.

The UN has been mocked for talking too much and doing too little, for passing resolutions but not seeing them carried out. Its machinery, which grew as more and more UN offices were opened all over the world, has been criticized as inefficient, wasteful, politically biased towards the poorer nations and out of touch with reality.

Developing nations say the UN does too little to help them, while **Western** nations grumble that they pay most but receive least. Critics also indicate that really important political decisions, such as arms reduction or peace enforcement, are taken not by the UN but by individual states acting on their own initiative. Although set up to preserve world peace, the UN itself has not stopped a single conflict.

The blue beret stands for peace, unity and hope – Canadian UN soldiers and Rwandan refugee children, 1994.

Successes

Most agree that the world would have been a far poorer and more dangerous place had the UN not existed. Although it cannot force states to act, at least it brings them together and sets them talking. Had it not called the Earth Summit and established the Kyoto Protocol, for example, a global environmental programme would have been almost unimaginable.

The UN's most valuable work is undertaken by its least glamorous agencies. Countless people are helped by its development programme and its **human rights** campaigning. The **World Bank** and the World Health Organization also do invaluable work under the UN umbrella.

Reform and the future

In 1997 Secretary-General Kofi Annan launched long overdue UN reform. Measures included establishing the post of deputy secretary-general, streamlining administration (for example, creating an Emergency Relief Coordinator for **humanitarian** assistance), cutting administrative costs and improving information activities better to explain the UN's work.

The changes were widely welcomed, especially by the USA, which had led criticism of UN wastefulness and bias. The UN emerged leaner and fitter. It needed to be. As if peacekeeping and tackling environmental problems and poverty were not enough, after 11 September 2001 it faced yet another challenge: global terrorism. Its response was swift and positive, but how effective it will be remains to be seen.

International terrorism – an old challenge returns. Damage to the Pentagon Building, Washington DC, USA, caused when a hijacked airliner was flown into it on 11 September 2001.

11 September 2001

A week after the terrorist attacks on New York and Washington DC, the UN General Assembly (which had been evacuated on 11 September) passed a resolution which included the following two clauses:
The General Assembly ...
• *strongly condemns the heinous acts of terrorism, which have caused enormous loss of human life, destruction and damage in the cities of New York, host city of the United Nations, and Washington DC ...*
• *urgently calls for international cooperation to prevent and eradicate acts of terrorism, and stresses that those responsible for aiding, supporting or harbouring the perpetrators, organizers and sponsors of such acts will be held accountable.*

Timeline

1919	League of Nations formed
1923	Corfu Incident shows League of Nations' weakness as a peacekeeper
1939	Outbreak of World War Two in Europe (to 1945)
1941	Atlantic Charter suggests the idea of a United Nations
1944	Dumbarton Oaks (USA) meeting sets out blueprint of UN
1945	UN founded, San Francisco
	UNESCO established
1946	General Assembly (51 members) first meets, London
	Security Council first meets, London
	Trygve Lie first secretary-general
	East versus West Cold War beginning
	Court of International Justice set up
	UN moves to New York
1948	UN mission to Palestine
	World Health Organization set up
	General Assembly accepts Universal Declaration of Human Rights
1949	UN brokers peace between Israel and Arabs
1950	Security Council agrees on UN intervention in aid of South Korea
	Beginning of Korean War (to 1953)
	UNICEF set up
1953	Dag Hammarskjöld becomes secretary-general
1955	Sixteen new member states accepted
1956	General Assembly sets up first UN peacekeeping force for Suez
1959	UN organizes treaty banning nuclear weapons from Antarctica
1960	UN troops sent to Congo
1961	U Thant becomes secretary-general
1962	World Food Programme established
1964	UN force sent to Cyprus
1965	Security Council membership rises to 15
1969	UN Fund for Population Activities set up
1971	People's Republic of China replaces Taiwan as China's UN representative
1972	Kurt Waldheim becomes secretary-general
1973	UN force sent to Middle East
1974	UN Special Committee Against Apartheid established
1978	UN force sent to Lebanon
1982	Javier Pérez de Cuéllar becomes secretary-general
1983	World Commission on Environment and Development founded
1984	USA leaves UNESCO
1987	Montreal Protocol on phasing out gases that damage the Earth's ozone layer
1988	UN forces sent to Afghanistan-Pakistan and Iran-Iraq

1990	Iraq invades Kuwait: UN-approved coalition against Iraq: Gulf War (to 1991)
1992	Boutros Boutros-Ghali becomes secretary-general
	Earth Summit in Rio de Janeiro
	UN force enters former Yugoslavia
	UN force sent to Cambodia
1993	UN missions to Uganda-Rwanda, Georgia and Haiti
1995	UN Conference on Women, Beijing, China
1997	Kofi Annan becomes secretary-general
	Widespread reform of UN started
	Kyoto Protocol on global warming drawn up
1998	UN enforcement troops sent to East Timor
2001	Terrorist attack on New York and Washington DC
	UN backs America's 'war on terrorism'

Further reading

Books

The UN publishes its own handbook, *Basic Facts*, which is regularly updated.

A Citizen's Guide to the World Community, Sean Connolly, Heinemann Library, 2002

Deliver Us from Evil, William Shawcross, Bloomsbury, 2001

A History of the United Nations, 2 vols, Edward Luard, Macmillan, 1982 & 1989

The United Nations, Stewart Ross, Wayland, 1989

The United Nations and International Politics, Stephen Ryan, Palgrave Macmillan, 2000

The United Nations: How it Works and What it Does, Edward Luard, Macmillan, 1994

United Nations in the Contemporary World, David J. Whittaker, Routledge, 1997

United Nations - Keeping the Peace, Sean Connolly, Heinemann Library, 2001

Unvanquished, Boutros Boutros-Ghali, I.B. Tauris, 1999

Websites

The UN has an excellent network of websites that can be accessed through
www.un.org

Some agencies offer excellent educational material, for example on human rights:
www.unhchr.ch/hredu.nsf

Individual countries have their own UN pages, for example:
www.una-uk.org
www.una-usa.org
www.australiaun.org

Glossary

Allied powers countries (including the UK, France, the USA and the USSR) who fought together against Germany, Italy and Japan during World War Two (1939–45)

annexed taken over by an adjoining territory, often without consultation

arbitration process of judging a case by an arbitrator

arbitrator someone accepted by groups in dispute to make a judgement in their case

boycotting refusing to have dealings with an organization or state

British Commonwealth association (founded in 1931) of the United Kingdom and some formerly British-controlled territories. In 1945 its members were the UK, Australia, Canada, Irish Free State, Newfoundland, New Zealand and South Africa.

capitalist based on an economic system in which land, factories and other ways of producing goods are owned and controlled by individuals, not the government

CNN Cable News Network, a US-based news and media organization

coercive using force

colonies territories governed by another country

communist someone who follows, or a description of, communism, a political movement which aims to create a classless society in which the means of production are owned in common

convention agreement between states

corruption dishonest behaviour by people in public office

crimes against humanity wrongs against whole or parts of a population

democratic conforming to the principles of rule by the people, in which government is carried out by representatives elected by the public

dictator ruler with absolute authority

disarmament giving up of, or a reduction in, armed forces or weapons

economic sanctions measures taken to prevent trade with a particular country

epidemic disease that is passed around between large numbers of people

free trade economic system that allows people to trade with as little government interference or control as possible

genocide killing of a large number of people

human rights conditions deserved by all human beings, such as freedom, equality or justice

humanitarian promoting the well-being and social rights of humans

infantry division large military unit of soldiers trained to fight on foot

International Monetary Fund international organization of 183 member countries founded in 1946 to establish monetary cooperation and stability, promote economic growth and employment and provide temporary financial assistance to individual countries

left-wing pursuing political change to gain greater freedom for ordinary people

mediate help sort out differences

nationalization making an industry the property of a nation

Nazi member of, or describing, the German National Socialist Workers' Party, a racist, violent and anti-democratic political group, which ruled Germany from 1933–45

nuclear weapons weapons whose destructive power comes from an uncontrolled nuclear reaction

ozone gas that forms a layer in the Earth's upper atmosphere, blocking most of the Sun's ultra-violet radiation

pacific rejecting the use of force

People's Republic of China name of the communist state of mainland China since 1949

proliferation rapid increase in numbers

protocol records of what was said and agreed at a conference

radicals people who desire extreme political or social changes

refugees people who flee from their country to another

republic country in which power rests with the people and their elected representatives

right-wing favoring strong government and opposing changes to the traditional social order

Russian Federation country formed in 1991 from the remains of the USSR after Ukraine, Belarus, Moldova and the Soviet republics in central Asia and the Baltic became independent

superpower major world power, usually referring to the USA and the USSR, 1945-91

sustainable development using resources without depleting or damaging them

Third World developing nations of the world

treaty negotiated agreement between countries

tribunal type of law court

unanimous having the consent of all parties

USSR Union of Soviet Socialist Republics; until its collapse in 1990, a communist superpower dominated by Russia

veto power to prohibit action by others

weapons of mass destruction weapons, such as nuclear or chemical weapons, that can kill whole populations

West the non-communist countries of Europe and America

Western term describing the democratic nations of North America and Western Europe

World Bank UN organization established to assist world economic development primarily through loans

Index